THE

CINNAMON

STORY

*Competitive
differentiation
when you MUST
win the sale*

BY TERRY SLATTERY

The Cinnamon Story
by Terry Slattery

Published by Slattery Sales Group Minneapolis, MN
www.slatterysales.com

Book design and layout: Ingenuity Marketing Group, LLC.

ISBN-13: 978-1-7320827-0-0
ISBN-13: 978-1-7320827-1-7

ifferentiating Value

The Emotional vs Logical Customer

Consequences

. Ask the Right Questions

ifferentiating Value

he Emotional vs. Logical Customer

onsequences

ny questions?"

ll I have are questions," he said.

That's perfect because that's our last step." I wrote:

. *Ask the right questions*

watched Avery's face to see if he was on board with me. His eyes had a

n interest and the kind of hunger that makes for a great sales person. "Let's

" he said.

Introduction

For over 30 years, I've led a management consulting and training organization headquartered in Minneapolis. We provide business leaders with tools and processes to help them grow their business through more effective competitive differentiation. This book shares a concept with you that has helped businesses increase their margins and top line revenue while keeping valued, profitable customer relationships for a longer period of time. The concept is "Differentiating Value" (DV).

We will show you:
- how to identify your real DV
- how to use it in conversations with your customers and prospects about your value
- how you can leverage your DV to increase profits and help grow your business

We work with organizations that have a small sales force and we work with those with hundreds of salespeople. Whether it's a large or small company, long or a short sales cycle, a big ticket or small ticket, a complex sale or simple transactional sale, tangible or intangible, effective use of DV helps to protect margins, reduce sales cycle time, and retain valued client relationships.

The Cinnamon Story demonstrates how DV can alter a customer's evaluation and decision processes to favor you.

When you have worked with over 2,100 organizations in 30 years, you have hundreds of great stories. We selected this story to share with you because it is dirt-simple, yet the principles apply to even the most complex sale.

CHAPTER 1

The Cinnamon Story

One day, Avery Davis, one of our long-term coaching clients, came into our office looking like he'd just lost his best friend. Avery was a very smart guy and usually great at sales.

I'd been at my desk going over my schedule, but I pushed that aside and asked him, "What's going on?"

He slumped down in the chair across from me and said, "I lost my biggest customer. They've been with me for ten years and they went to another supplier because they could buy cinnamon from that other supplier at three cents per pound lower than I could sell it to them. Three cents! How do I get this customer back?"

My response was: "Maybe you can't."

Avery came back with, "I didn't pay you the kind of money you're charging to tell me that. How do I get them back?"

I got up and walked around my desk to stand in front of Avery. I'd seen this kind of pain a lot in my decades of coaching sales people—and I'd felt it plenty myself.

I wanted to be sure I had his attention. He watched me lean back against the edge of the desk.

Then, I held up three fingers. "You won't get them back until you can answer these questions:

'What's going to happen because th[...]
Who's it going to happen to?
And how will what's going to happen [...]

"I don't know how to answer that," [...]
"Tell me about this customer."
"They're a food products produce[...] cinnamon for about ten years. They rece[...] called me and said that even though we've [...] and he's never had a problem, he saw that [...] more for our cinnamon than he could get fr[...]

Avery shifted in his chair, rubbed a ha[...] continued, "This new buyer said that out o[...] relationship, he wanted to give me a chance to [...] he was going to move the business."

"How did you differentiate against that low[...] asked.

"I told him about the benefits of working with [...] quality cinnamon. We sell the cinnamon in small b[...] have to buy big quantities and risk the cinnamon not [...] Our service and support is great."

"What did this buyer say?"

"He just kept coming back to three cents a pound."

"And you lost the business?"

"Just this morning. I need you to help me get them ba[...]

"All right. I know you have a very high differentiatin[...] worked on it in bootcamps and coaching. And you kno[...] pushed you to compete on price, rather than competing on [...] not having your DV. That's what we've got to get back to and [...] show you how to do it."

Going to the whiteboard that stretches across most of one [...] office, I wrote:

CHAPTER 2

The Origins and Logic of Differentiating Value

"**D**o you remember what you learned about Differentiating Value, or DV, in the sales bootcamp?" As I asked this to Avery, I went to my door, intending to tell my admin that I'd be busy for the next few hours.

Avery rubbed his chin and said, "I remember you saying that an iron law of the marketplace is that every competitor has to bring a differentiating value or they're stuck competing on price. But I thought I did that. I told the buyer all about our quality and freshness."

Through the open door of my office, I saw another client of ours, Maria Rossi, talking with my admin. I'd just been helping Maria clarify her DV message last week and I knew she'd been struggling with proposals lately. She was probably here to schedule a coaching session with me as a lot of my clients did when they got stuck.

From the doorway, I asked, "Maria, we're talking about DV and the sales process, do you want to join us?"

"Of course!" she said. I introduced her to Avery and he explained the bind he was in. Her face grew serious as she listened. As a partner in an online marketing firm, Maria was always fighting price pressure in a highly competitive marketplace. Her firm worked with professional services companies to create lead-generating websites and manage powerful online reputations.

Recently, she'd been coming to me for help because her prospects kept going dark in the middle of the sales process. They'd switch from seeming excited about what her firm could offer to not responding to her calls and emails.

To solve her problem, and Avery's, we had to start with the core of Differentiating Value.

I closed my door and went back to the front of my desk, asking, "Maria, the quality of your services is better than your competitors, isn't it?"

"Measurably better," she said.

"Why don't you tell your prospect that in the sales process?"

"Quality is just table stakes," she said. "You taught me that. If I want to stand out from the competition, really differentiate what my firm can do, I have to show a prospect what's unique about working with us, or how we execute, in ways that are demonstrably better. Plus, I have to pick uniqueness or execution that the prospect will value. I can't just say what's important to my firm. Prospects don't care."

I went to the white board and wrote: *Differentiate – a difference that distinguishes.* I said, "You're right—that's the starting point."

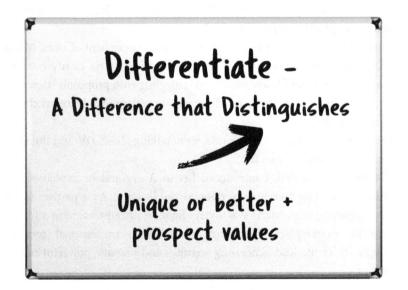

CHAPTER 2

The Origins and Logic of Differentiating Value

"**D**o you remember what you learned about Differentiating Value, or DV, in the sales bootcamp?" As I asked this to Avery, I went to my door, intending to tell my admin that I'd be busy for the next few hours.

Avery rubbed his chin and said, "I remember you saying that an iron law of the marketplace is that every competitor has to bring a differentiating value or they're stuck competing on price. But I thought I did that. I told the buyer all about our quality and freshness."

Through the open door of my office, I saw another client of ours, Maria Rossi, talking with my admin. I'd just been helping Maria clarify her DV message last week and I knew she'd been struggling with proposals lately. She was probably here to schedule a coaching session with me as a lot of my clients did when they got stuck.

From the doorway, I asked, "Maria, we're talking about DV and the sales process, do you want to join us?"

"Of course!" she said. I introduced her to Avery and he explained the bind he was in. Her face grew serious as she listened. As a partner in an online marketing firm, Maria was always fighting price pressure in a highly competitive marketplace. Her firm worked with professional services companies to create lead-generating websites and manage powerful online reputations.

Recently, she'd been coming to me for help because her prospects kept going dark in the middle of the sales process. They'd switch from seeming excited about what her firm could offer to not responding to her calls and emails.

To solve her problem, and Avery's, we had to start with the core of Differentiating Value.

I closed my door and went back to the front of my desk, asking, "Maria, the quality of your services is better than your competitors, isn't it?"

"Measurably better," she said.

"Why don't you tell your prospect that in the sales process?"

"Quality is just table stakes," she said. "You taught me that. If I want to stand out from the competition, really differentiate what my firm can do, I have to show a prospect what's unique about working with us, or how we execute, in ways that are demonstrably better. Plus, I have to pick uniqueness or execution that the prospect will value. I can't just say what's important to my firm. Prospects don't care."

I went to the white board and wrote: *Differentiate – a difference that distinguishes.* I said, "You're right—that's the starting point."

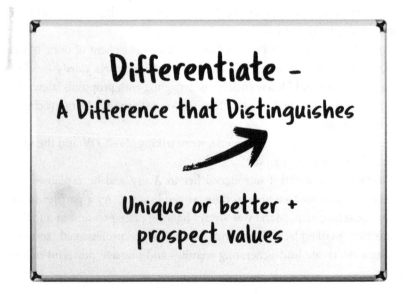

CHAPTER 1

The Cinnamon Story

One day, Avery Davis, one of our long-term coaching clients, came into our office looking like he'd just lost his best friend. Avery was a very smart guy and usually great at sales.

I'd been at my desk going over my schedule, but I pushed that aside and asked him, "What's going on?"

He slumped down in the chair across from me and said, "I lost my biggest customer. They've been with me for ten years and they went to another supplier because they could buy cinnamon from that other supplier at three cents per pound lower than I could sell it to them. Three cents! How do I get this customer back?"

My response was: "Maybe you can't."

Avery came back with, "I didn't pay you the kind of money you're charging to tell me that. How do I get them back?"

I got up and walked around my desk to stand in front of Avery. I'd seen this kind of pain a lot in my decades of coaching sales people—and I'd felt it plenty myself.

I wanted to be sure I had his attention. He watched me lean back against the edge of the desk.

Then, I held up three fingers. "You won't get them back until you can answer these questions:

Introduction

For over 30 years, I've led a management consulting and training organization headquartered in Minneapolis. We provide business leaders with tools and processes to help them grow their business through more effective competitive differentiation. This book shares a concept with you that has helped businesses increase their margins and top line revenue while keeping valued, profitable customer relationships for a longer period of time. The concept is "Differentiating Value" (DV).

We will show you:
- how to identify your real DV
- how to use it in conversations with your customers and prospects about your value
- how you can leverage your DV to increase profits and help grow your business

We work with organizations that have a small sales force and we work with those with hundreds of salespeople. Whether it's a large or small company, long or a short sales cycle, a big ticket or small ticket, a complex sale or simple transactional sale, tangible or intangible, effective use of DV helps to protect margins, reduce sales cycle time, and retain valued client relationships.

The Cinnamon Story demonstrates how DV can alter a customer's evaluation and decision processes to favor you.

When you have worked with over 2,100 organizations in 30 years, you have hundreds of great stories. We selected this story to share with you because it is dirt-simple, yet the principles apply to even the most complex sale.

'What's going to happen because they are not buying cinnamon from you?

Who's it going to happen to?

And how will what's going to happen show up in their life?'"

"I don't know how to answer that," he said.

"Tell me about this customer."

"They're a food products producer and I've been selling them cinnamon for about ten years. They recently promoted a new buyer. He called me and said that even though we've been giving him great service and he's never had a problem, he saw that we charge three cents a pound more for our cinnamon than he could get from a competitor."

Avery shifted in his chair, rubbed a hand across his forehead and continued, "This new buyer said that out of respect for the ten-year relationship, he wanted to give me a chance to match that lower price or he was going to move the business."

"How did you differentiate against that lower price competitor?" I asked.

"I told him about the benefits of working with us. We have very high quality cinnamon. We sell the cinnamon in small batches so they didn't have to buy big quantities and risk the cinnamon not being fresh enough. Our service and support is great."

"What did this buyer say?"

"He just kept coming back to three cents a pound."

"And you lost the business?"

"Just this morning. I need you to help me get them back."

"All right. I know you have a very high differentiating value. We've worked on it in bootcamps and coaching. And you know this buyer pushed you to compete on price, rather than competing on the value of not having your DV. That's what we've got to get back to and I'm going to show you how to do it."

Going to the whiteboard that stretches across most of one wall of my office, I wrote:

```
1. Differentiating Value

2. The Emotional vs Logical Customer

3. Consequences

4. Ask the Right Questions
```

1. *Differentiating Value*
2. *The Emotional vs. Logical Customer*
3. *Consequences*

"Any questions?"

"All I have are questions," he said.

"That's perfect because that's our last step." I wrote:

4. *Ask the right questions*

I watched Avery's face to see if he was on board with me. His eyes had a keen interest and the kind of hunger that makes for a great sales person. "Let's go," he said.

I also wrote: *Unique or better + Prospect values.*

Circling the plus sign, I told Avery, "This is your differentiating value."

"Ah, you're saying that my buyer doesn't value freshness enough for it to be on his radar and that quality doesn't distinguish me from my competitors. But then, what does?"

"What's your differentiating value?" I asked Maria.

She got a gleam in her eye and said, "How important is it to you that your new website launch on time?"

I laughed because I'd taught Maria to phrase her DV as a series of questions. I'd get to that point with Avery soon, but first we needed to understand the fundamental concept of DV itself.

Maria understood that I was setting her up by asking for her DV as a statement. She gamely went on to say, "In my office, internally, we say our DV is the integrity of our project delivery, we know how to get things done, and because we offer integrated solutions, we deliver results our clients can easily measure. We even help them put the tracking in place."

"I know I put you in a corner asking you to say it as a statement rather than questions, like I taught you," I told her. "Consider that putting the tracking in place is still table-stakes, entry-level quality. It's the fact that you help them use it effectively that differentiates your company."

"But I am selling a commodity," Avery said. "It's physically the same cinnamon and everyone can get it at around the same price. How do I get around that?"

"Price isn't the same as cost," I told him. "Let me explain."

CHAPTER 3

Cost vs. Price

I went to a clear area on the whiteboard and wrote the word "Cost" with the word "Price" above it. I drew a line linking the two.

"Any economist will tell you that price is a component of cost," I told Avery. "But our prospects and buyers love to conflate or intermingle price and cost. If you let them get away with that, you'll find your margins evaporate."

With a smile, I said, "Now, if you want to sell on price, that conflation is your friend. But if you're selling based on value, you have to master distinguishing cost from price. If you can't handle that conversation effectively, you're going to lose nearly every time to someone else's solution that is lower priced, but has a higher cost in the long run."

"Can I ever get that business back once I've lost it?" Avery asked. He sat forward in his chair, elbows on knees, looking back and forth from me to the whiteboard.

"Oh yes," I answered. "I saw this recently in a manufacturing application. An ultra high-value supplier lost business because the buyer based their decision on the price of the parts – and my high-value client's price was about 40% higher than the low-price provider. Guess what happened?"

"Your client got a call back," Maria said with a wry grin. "This happens to me, too. The client doesn't realize, going in, how costly a delay is going to be, or how costly it is not to have the right fit and expertise."

I nodded to her. "You got it. A few months later, the high-value player got a call. It turned out that this low-price vendor could not deliver on time. The buyer had saved $100,000 a year up front, but now the delivery delay was pushing back the launch of a new product line. In fact, it had already pushed back the launch date by 300 days. Lost time to market was costing this company $1.5 million per day. The low-price vendor was the highest-cost vendor. The cost of saving that $100,000 was hundreds of millions of dollars in lost revenue."

"Did they switch back to the high-value, low-cost provider?" Avery asked.

"They did. My client is their supplier now. They're on schedule and the decision-maker who selected that initial low price, high cost provider is now 'free to pursue other business opportunities,' as they said to explain that executive's speedy departure."

I wrote on the whiteboard: *Price ≠ Cost!*

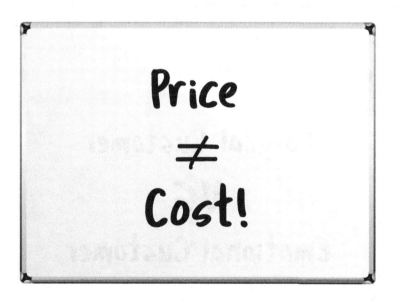

CHAPTER 4

Emotional vs. Logical Customer

W e'd been talking about prospective clients and customers by their job labels (buyer, product-line manager and so on), but there was a more useful way to describe them. I wanted to make sure that Avery and Maria were clear about this before I sent them out into the world to work on communicating their DV.

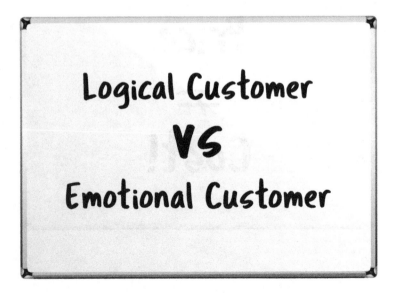

On the whiteboard I wrote: *Logical Customer vs. Emotional Customer*

"These are the two roles we see in every complex sale," I told them. "If the selling team does not recognize and leverage these roles, they run the risk of conceding their DV, being treated as a commodity and forced to compete on price. Do you know who is which kind of customer?"

"I think my buyer is the Logical Customer," Avery said. "So I have to find the Emotional Customer?"

I said, "Exactly. Now, we use the term 'Logical Customer' not because this person is behaving in a particularly logical way. As you saw from price vs. cost, they might make some very illogical decisions. We call them the Logical Customer because they're the logical point of entry for a salesperson who hasn't thought very deeply about the process of selling and doesn't mind competing on price. You're in for a hard life if you do not recognize that the Logical Customer is not your friend, unless your business model is low price."

I wrote on the whiteboard: *Attributes of the Logical Customer.*

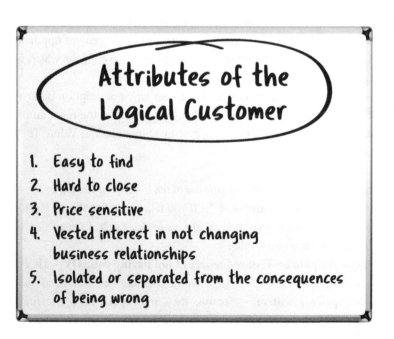

Attributes of the Logical Customer

1. Easy to find
2. Hard to close
3. Price sensitive
4. Vested interest in not changing business relationships
5. Isolated or separated from the consequences of being wrong

Under that I listed the attributes, explaining them as I went.

1. **Easy to find** – Every competitor you have is already calling on them, because they are easy to find. They get paid to talk to salespeople.
2. **Hard to close** – They usually have a limited scope of authority and can't make a decision without someone else's approval.
3. **Price sensitive** – Because price concessions are one of the few areas they can influence, they get paid to conflate price and cost, and they're bonused based on concessions from vendors.
4. **Vested interest in not changing business relationships** – Because they get nothing for going through it except an occasional plaque.
5. **Isolated or separated from the consequences of being wrong** – They're also isolated from the consequences of delay while they extract price concessions.

Avery pointed at the words I'd written, saying, "Seeing that, my cinnamon buyer is definitely the Logical Customer."

"And when your sales efforts are focused on the Logical Customer because it's habitual or comfortable for the sales people, I promise that your margins are under unnecessary pressure. You have a margin enhancement opportunity," I said, making sure that Maria was also in the game, even if she wasn't facing the squeeze Avery was right now.

I went on to explain, "Emotional Customer isn't a description of how they think or behave. It refers to the fact that they would be the most emotional about the consequences of not having your Differentiating Value. They feel the pain."

I wrote on the whiteboard: *Attributes of the Emotional Customer*

1. **Zero interest in your "stuff"** – If you talk to the Emotional Customers about your stuff, they will send you to the Logical Customer, where price always trumps value.
2. **Feels the pain and consequences of not having your DV** – This might be time to market, ability to deliver to their customers, and so on.
3. **Not price sensitive** – Because they are experiencing the financial, operational or market-share consequences of not having your

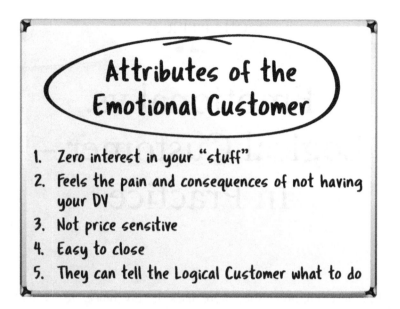

Attributes of the Emotional Customer

1. Zero interest in your "stuff"
2. Feels the pain and consequences of not having your DV
3. Not price sensitive
4. Easy to close
5. They can tell the Logical Customer what to do

Differentiating Value, your price premium looks reasonable compared to the consequences of not having your DV.

4. Easy to close – They're the ones getting the bill for not having you. Your sales cycles are shorter when you focus on the Emotional Customers.

5. They can tell the Logical Customer what to do – This is the one that endears them to you the most. If they know they need you, they can make it happen.

I closed by saying, "In sales, we operate in an economic democracy, which means the one who has the biggest consequences gets the most votes, providing they have the Emotional Customer (or at least their agenda) at the table."

It was getting late in the day. "Why don't we resume this tomorrow," I told them. "Tonight and tomorrow morning, I want you to work on identifying the Emotional and Logical Customers for sales you're currently engaged in. Avery, work on that company you want to renew your cinnamon contract. Maria, pick a big one you're working on now. Come back after lunch tomorrow and let me know who each player is."

CHAPTER 5

Emotional vs.
Logical Customer –
In Practice

The next afternoon they were back in my office. Avery looked triumphant while Maria seemed perplexed. Avery and Maria took the seats across from my desk. I leaned against my desk in front of them.

"What happened?" I asked.

"I found the Emotional Customer!" Avery said. "I met with him this morning and he's going to talk to the buyer."

That sounded like great news, but I wasn't convinced. I motioned for Avery to go on.

"I called the main food scientist I work with. He's the one who has to figure out formulations for new products. They do a lot of generics, so when a major brand comes out with a new product, he goes nose to the grindstone to figure out what's in it and how to copy it. He puts in a lot of long hours, and for the last eight years he's been relying on my people to come in and help him out. We've got some real taste experts at my company. They shave days off his process."

"How do you know he's the Emotional Customer?" I asked.

"He got so angry when I told him that the buyer had switched companies. I mean, he was furious."

"Remember, Emotional Customer doesn't mean that they get emotional. Does he fit the attributes?" I pointed at the whiteboard where the attributes of both the Logical and Emotional Customers were still listed from yesterday's conversation.

EMOTIONAL CUSTOMER

1. Zero interest in your "stuff"
2. Feels the pain and consequences of not having your DV
3. Not price sensitive
4. Easy to close
5. They can tell the Logical Customer what to do

"Well, he cares some about the cinnamon being fresh, but not nearly as much as he does about having our help. He definitely feels the pain. He doesn't care about price and he was super easy to close." Avery frowned and twisted his hands together. He looked down and admitted, "He can't tell the buyer what to do. He can complain, but he can't actually make him choose our company."

"Who does this food scientist report to?" I asked.

"The executive in charge of all the cereal generics: the product line manager. She's his boss."

"Can she tell the buyer to choose you?"

"Yes."

"Then we've found your Emotional Customer. She's the one you need to talk to about the consequences to the company of not using your company as their cinnamon supplier." I turned to Maria and asked, "What about you, Maria? Did you find your Emotional Customer?"

"I thought it was the Shareholder in charge of marketing," she said, but she shook her head as she talked. "We're talking to a mid-sized financial services firm, with regional marketing managers and a national marketing director on a marketing committee. So I assumed the members of the marketing committee were the Emotional Customers."

She stood and walked to the whiteboard, standing near the spot that said:

LOGICAL CUSTOMER

1. Easy to find
2. Hard to close
3. Price sensitive
4. Vested interest in not changing business relationships
5. Isolated or separated from the consequences of being wrong

"But then I realized that the reason the people on the marketing committee, those regional and national marketing people, are dragging their feet about the solution we want to implement is that they're very price sensitive and they don't want to change. My marketing firm wants to give them the best online presence, but they're focused on price."

Maria pointed at #3 and #4, then moved her finger down to #5. "This one too," she said. "It doesn't matter if they're using outdated technology and old marketing strategies. If they don't get a lot of new leads, they don't feel pain from it, their jobs aren't on the line. And the problem is, this is also true for the Marketing Director. He's just supposed to make sure marketing runs smoothly. He doesn't feel the pinch if online leads are being driven away by their old website or dropped because they don't know how to nurture them."

"He's isolated from the long-term consequences," I pointed out. "It's easy for the Marketing Director and the regional managers to think things are working well enough. It might even be risky to their jobs if an outsider like you can come in and do it better than they're doing it. The Marketing Director might even be the one stalling your proposal after the initial meetings. Now, who is feeling the pain of not hiring your firm?"

"The firm shareholders who want to retire in a few years. They'll have trouble getting the price they want for their part of the firm if the firm isn't growing," she said. Maria's expression changed with clarity replacing confusion and she went on to say, "You know, I wonder if we could attach a growth percentage to the poor performance of their current, outdated system. If I could show them that they could grow even three or four percent faster over the next few years, they would immediately get what that means for their ability to hire the best talent and sell their stake in the firm when they want, and for the price they want."

"You've got it."

"We've been going at it all wrong. No wonder we're bogged down. I could offer a short, private webinar for the firm's stakeholders about leadership transitions—they always want to talk about that—and include how the right marketing software, implemented well by us, eases the transition and increases the price for their stake in the firm."

CHAPTER 6

Your DV Erodes Over Time

Maria walked back to her chair and sat, asking me, "Now that I know who I need to be talking to, how do I know if I have a problem with my DV? I want to make sure I'm getting the right message to the right people."

"Great question," I told her. "One of the first places you'll feel it is in pressure on margins, especially sudden, undue pressure. Have you ever been surprised at the last minute in a long, complex sale?"

"Have I? All the time. In the industries we work with, it's usually new decision makers coming in – either they're new to the organization, or the people we were working with didn't disclose their involvement." She looked over at Avery and asked, "What about your industry?"

He rubbed a hand through his hair and the set of his mouth looked grim. I knew he'd been feeling the squeeze with more clients than just the one that had dropped him yesterday.

"New competitors happen fairly often," he admitted. "Sometimes it's new or additional decision makers, or we have the same decision makers but they got handed, or have developed, a new set of ground rules for making the buying decision. We end up scrambling and even if we get the sale, our gross margins have been diminished so much we don't know if it was worth it."

I nodded. "Surprises in the sales process almost always put you at a disadvantage. What you're both describing happens when the sales team running the pursuit of the sale hasn't had enough contact with the Emotional Customer. It usually means you didn't ask the Logical Customer enough questions to pull the Emotional Customer's agenda into the evaluation and decision process."

I drew a triangle on the whiteboard, showing the decline of relationships toward commodity.

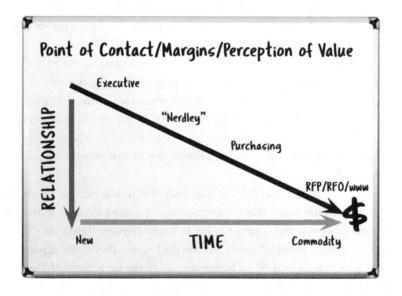

"If you don't manage relationships properly, they always decline to commodity. When a relationship is new, you look different, innovative, exciting. Your point of contact, your margins and the prospect's perception of your value are at their absolute peak early in the relationship. Avery, what was this like for you early on with your cinnamon buyer?"

"Great! We met members of the executive team and they were really excited about the solutions we had. They knew they had problems getting generics to market fast enough and they were eager for us to get to work."

"It's similar for us," Maria said, leaning back in her chair with her fingers steepled in front of her, mouth set in a line. "We meet owners of the firm early on, but they're very busy so after a few months they're not that interested in talking to us and leave us to work with the marketing people."

I wrote "Executive" at the top of the relationship triangle. "What's happened is that within the company, problems have been elevated to the executive level. That's why they're bringing in a new vendor or service provider. They haven't been able to solve the problems by themselves or with their existing vendors. It's easy to get to the executive level when you're bringing a solution to a problem that's on that executive's list of things to fix—especially if it's been there for a long time. The net effect is that you are at a high level of contact and you are not going to be competing primarily on price. Your margins are better because their perception of your value is high."

I moved down the slope of the triangle. "Time passes and as you're working through the relationship and delivering new results for them, some of your expertise is transferred from you to the customer. That's what they paid you for and it's inevitable. Chances are the executive who is the real decision maker either brought in an expert or trained an expert in whatever you do, and passed off responsibility for the relationship to that expert. We call that expert 'Nerdley.'"

I wrote the name "Nerdley" at the midpoint in the decline down the line from margins and value to commodity. "It comes time to renew the relationship because the contract is up, but now Nerdley thinks they know more than you do about whatever it is you do, because they're the experts."

"Oh wow," Maria said. "This happens to us all the time. Honestly, in two-thirds of my contract renewals I'm fighting my way through that Nerdley point. It's awful. A firm will hire some kid out of college, have us train them, and suddenly they think they know more about online marketing than our company, even though we have decades of experience and work with firms like theirs across the country, solving problems more complex than they've ever seen."

"We liked working with the experts at our cinnamon buyer," Avery said. "But we did run into the same problem. With what they've learned from us, they've shaved a few days off the generic product development cycle, so it looks like we're less valuable now."

I tapped the executive level and then Nerdley on the whiteboard. "Yes, you're at a lower point of contact and Nerdley's perception of your value is less. That will be reflected in the margins on the renewal. Guess what happens the next time your contract comes up for renewal?"

Looking disheartened, Avery pointed at the lower end of the triangle. "Is there someone under Nerdley?"

"There is. You've gone another one, two, three years in this relationship. You're delivering your product or services, but you're not making as much money as you used to. And now that it's time to renew again, Nerdley might be busy working on other projects. They're the expert, maybe they've been promoted internally. Now you find yourself talking to somebody in purchasing or supply chain, commodity sourcing, and so on.

"Notice what happened: You started with the Emotional Customer and now you've slipped down to the ultimate Logical Customer. When working with purchasing, you're so far down the food chain that daylight doesn't get down there. Purchasing's perception of value is that no vendor has any. They will hammer the margins on your business until they are non-existent or razor thin."

"Does it get worse?" Maria asked.

"Yes, there's one stop left after purchasing. That last stop is where you don't get a chance to talk to a human being. Instead, you're directed to a website and asked to complete a spreadsheet questionnaire. You've become column fodder. This is where all the RFPs and RFQs are positioned.

"The good news at this point is that if you choose to compete at this level of business, in the commodity world, the last thing you need is a sales force, because most of the time you can get this type of business done with less expensive people."

Maria and Avery shared a grim look. Eliminating the sales force in their organizations would mean that Avery was out of a job and Maria would lose some of the work she enjoyed most: finding and bringing in exciting new clients.

CHAPTER 7

Doom
of Discounting

"You can see that the demands for price concessions typically come from the Logical Customer, starting with the slide to Nerdley here," I said, pointing at the diagram on the whiteboard. "Too often the salespeople do not understand that margins, the most precious dollars to the business, are the first casualty when there are price concessions."

Maria sighed and looked at Avery. They were both seller-doers for their businesses, which meant they had to both sell and deliver their products. This meant that they got to see both sides of the equation, but they also had salespeople who didn't understand this.

I told them, "I know you two understand it, but I want you to be able to take this back to the sales people at your companies. Let me show you how to demonstrate the negative impact of discounting. They'll see why the ability to defend your Differentiating Value is critical to maximum margins.

"Try this simple exercise with anyone in your sales force who consistently is asking for discounts when they're stuck down here selling to Nerdly. Ask them this question: how much additional volume would they need to sell at a given discount to get back the margin dollars the sales person wants to give away with the discount?"

I went to my desk and pulled out a page from a recent workshop. This sheet showed the doom of discounting and how dramatically sales had to increase to make up for modest discounts. I gave Avery and Maria each a copy.

"Compare your sales person's answer with the real one from this table. I'm going to warn you, this can lead to management depression, so don't do this survey at the end of a hard business day; do it in the morning when you're fresh and can handle it. The impact of this can be huge for you, your company and your sales people. They'll start to see how they could end up discounting themselves right out of a job."

THE DOOM OF DISCOUNTING

Normal % of profit on selling price	% price cut	% Increase in sales to make same dollar profit	Normal % of profit on selling price	% price cut	% Increase in sales to make same dollar profit
20%	5% 10% 15%	33% 100% 300%	**33.5%**	5% 10% 15% 20% 25%	18% 43% 81% 148% 294%
25%	5% 10% 15% 20%	25% 67% 150% 400%	**35%**	5% 10% 15% 20% 25%	17% 40% 75% 133% 250%
30%	5% 10% 15% 20% 25%	20% 50% 100% 200% 500%	**40%**	5% 10% 15% 20% 25%	14% 33% 60% 100% 167%

Before attempting to increase sales by discounting prices, do the math!

EXAMPLE

Sales $5,000
Margin of profit 25%
Gross profit 25% of $5,000 = $1,250
Proposed price cut 10%

New sales volume for $1,250 profit
$5,000 + 67% of $5,000 = $8,350

CHAPTER 8

The Logic of DV Comes in Two Flavors

Application of the Principles of DV to Your Business

"If I have the Emotional Customer in my sights, and I'm determined not to discount, how do I know if the problem is my DV itself or how I'm presenting it?" Avery asked.

"Clearly you're ready for this," I told him and went back to my desk for the DV worksheet I use with clients. I was enjoying this mini-workshop with two smart sales people who were up against some of the hardest challenges in complex sales. I gave each of them a copy of the DV worksheet.

"You both know that what you're offering is superior to your competition, but you're being pressured to discount in order to get business. That goes back to what we said about price vs. cost. The Logical Customer is often incentivized to get you to discount as much as you can. If you can't defend your superior offering by articulating your DV correctly, you will often wind up making disastrous price concessions."

I wrote on the whiteboard: *Unique, better.*

"DV refers to the things you do—and the results you create—that separate you from your competition. You want to identify what you do that is demonstrably better and has value. But there are a lot of pitfalls here. Why don't you two take a minute and fill out that first column," I suggested. "The one that asks, 'What are the top five strengths or unique characteristics you offer to your ideal prospect?'"

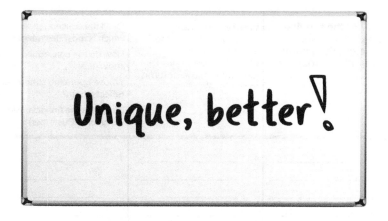

While they were working, I wrote on the whiteboard:
Quality
Service
Support
Great people
Local inventory
Well-trained employees
When they looked up, they both started laughing.
"Okay, I have three of those," Avery admitted.

What are the top five strengths or unique characteristics you offer to your ideal prospects?	What are all the consequences to the prospect in absence of each strength you identified in the column to the left?	Of all the consequences, which is most desirable? How do the consequences show up? Whose operating statement reflects them? Who gets the financial bill? (Emotional Customer)
1.	1.	1.
2.	2.	2.
3.	3.	3.
4.	4.	4.
5.	5.	5.

"And what happens when your competitors have similar lists and they all sound like you? As soon as you sound alike, prospects think 'oh good, a commodity' and the selection criteria is reduced to price."

"I listed four!" Maria said, still laughing. "And I've been through your bootcamp, Terry. But one of the keys I learned from the bootcamp is that your DV can start with these very similar sounding words and end up in an entirely different place. I do have great people at my firm, but I don't say that in the sales process and I don't say it on my website. It's part of our brand, but your brand isn't something you declare, it's what you demonstrate. So I have to show that I have great people and what it's like to work with them."

"Ah, I get it," Avery said. "My DV can start with the quality of the cinnamon and its freshness, and also that local inventory piece, that they can order small batches, and the expert service we give, but I can't stop there. Okay, what's next? I'm ready."

"Next we're going to want to turn your DV into consequences, but first, since we were just talking about the Logical and Emotional Customers, I want to prepare you for the Logical Customer to have objections," I said.

Since I was still standing at the whiteboard, I quickly wrote a list:

Common DV objections:
1. Don't have time
2. Cost is too high
3. Too hard to make the change

Common DV objections:

1. Don't have time

2. Cost too high

3. Too hard to make the change

"How often do you get these?" I asked.

"All the time," Maria said.

"All of these objections are straw men used by the Logical Customer to take the sale off track. They don't want to go through the pain of change," I explained. "I don't want you to think just because we've isolated your DV, and once we've identified consequences, that's it's a smooth slide into a sale. I don't want you blindsided when you're trying to position your DV and the consequences associated with not having it. No matter how well you do that, you still have to anticipate the Logical Customer is going to push back."

I pointed the marker in my hand at both of them, asking, "Other than the cinnamon buyer, who's already in the mix here, which one of you most recently had a Logical Customer try to derail your sales process?"

"I wrote a pretty great email and sent it to the person I think is the Emotional Customer on a deal we're trying to close, and it got forwarded to the Logical Customer who immediately took over and went back to price, does that count?" Maria asked.

"Absolutely. And what did you do?"

"I tried to talk about our DV, but I was thrown by it. I was talking instead of asking. I don't even know what to ask," she admitted.

I nodded, smiling a little. This was a very common situation. "Most people don't," I told her. "The first step is to remember that you're now talking to the Logical Customer and this is their nature. Then, step two, go back to the consequences to the Emotional Customer—even if you're still talking to the Logical Customer. Then package up a question like this, 'I realize you're busy and this may be an inconvenience. When you and (name the Emotional Customer) discussed the consequences, costs and delays, how comfortable were they with that impact on them?'"

Maria's face lit up. "That's great! Let's get to consequences so I can go back and use this in that sale!"

SUMMARY

Struggling to Find Your DV?

If you're still struggling to understand your DV, why not ask your best customers what they need from you and why they stay. They'll not only help you speed through the process of expressing your DV, but they'll create excitement and momentum internally because people at your company can see where they're being successful.

You can do this one-on-one or in small groups where your best customers tell stories about what you've done for them.

Being proactive and talking to your best customers is a fantastic way to review what's working and what isn't about your services or products. Do this at least annually or as products and services are added or updated.

Struggling with DV can also mean that you're too close to it. I frequently do half-day and full-day workshops with clients to define their DV, help them put it into questions, identify consequences and think through sales objections. I often find that clients think they have everything they need when they only have basic facts that won't communicate to the prospects in a way that closes sales.

In the following chapter, you'll learn about identifying consequences, but if you find yourself struggling to go deep on these, it might be time to give me a call.

CHAPTER 9

Turning the Absence
of Your DV Into
Consequences

I explained, "A big part of the problem, as you two just said, is the focus on talking about that left column. We've seen too many presentations and sales calls where the focus is on the left column, and you can watch the eyes of the audience glaze over and attention slips away. The problem is, these are what you want the prospect to value. It's about you and your great people—or you and your cinnamon. Guess what your prospects are really interested in?"

"Profits?" Avery asked.

"Success?" Maria tried.

"Maybe," I said. "But it's a sure bet they're always interested in themselves. You have to manage the translation from your stuff, your cinnamon, your people, your delivery system, to the consequences to the customer of them not having your cinnamon. The consequences are the real-world expression of your DV—or not having it."

Here's why they won't do the translation for themselves from the left column to the consequences:

1. They're not motivated. They think you're a commodity and over-priced and they are doing fine without you.

2. They don't have the same level of expertise that you do in understanding the consequences.

"Think about it. All of us who sell have solved similar problems for customers hundreds of times that this prospect may only face very few times in their careers. Our experience is greater. Only you can translate from facts and features to the consequences of not having the way you do things."

"That's so true," Avery said. "My cinnamon buyer doesn't realize that we've been working with food developers for decades and we've amassed a huge storehouse of experience and knowledge. That's why we can shave so much time off their development process."

Maria was nodding as he talked. She said, "It's a little easier to show in my industry because we can point to benchmarks and our experience with similar implementations. We can say: 'here's the industry average and here's what we produce,' but we still get Nerdley and other people trying to put us in a bucket with firms that don't deliver like we do."

I explained, "Talking about benchmarks and experience isn't the same as showing the consequences—there must be consequences to the prospective customer for not doing business with you. There are consequences of not having access to your Differentiating Value."

I wrote on the whiteboard: *It's always about the consequences.*

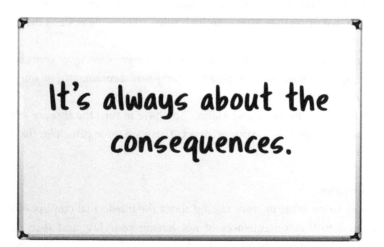

It's always about the consequences.

> **A sale is made in every meeting or conversation with prospects. Either they convince you that you're a commodity, or you prove you're not.**

"As we've seen, those consequences might not be experienced by the people you're talking to—the Logical Customers. So we have to look at effective ways to put your real value into play. But I've got to warn you, when you start to implement this, customers and prospects are still going to work hard to convince you that you have no Differentiating Value. They want to remove any risk they'd have in taking the low price, low value vendor by forcing you to match that price; they want your high value at the same price as the lowest price competitor."

I wrote on the whiteboard: *A sale is made in every meeting or conversation with prospects. Either they convince you that you're a commodity, or you prove you're not.*

I turned back to Avery and Maria. "You have to turn the absence of your DV into consequences to your prospect. There are three principles that help you do this:

1. Translation

"Translation takes us from talking about the intellectual concept of your cinnamon to the consequences of not having your DV, and then to the emotional basis for a decision—the decision to change either behavior or business relationships.

2. Isolation

"Isolation refers to the distance between a Logical Customer's price-based decision and its consequences. It shows up when you talk to the people in purchasing. As we've seen, the real consequences of not having your DV don't show up in purchasing—they show up in engineering, marketing, sales or customer service."

"Often this is what's happening when you've got a really strong business case—it makes economic and business sense—but the prospect won't pull the trigger. Or they're taking forever to make a decision. The reason for the delay is usually the isolation between the person who makes the decision and those who will experience the consequences of not having your DV."

3. Core Competencies

"Maria, this is what you mentioned yesterday. These are the table stakes or the minimum characteristics a vendor must have to be seriously considered. If you have DV and an appropriately high price, you must be prepared to influence the prospect's decision process away from price and core competencies and toward DV. When articulated correctly, the consequences of not having your DV can trump core competencies and lower-priced competition."

SUMMARY

What most people think are differentiators are really just table stakes, or mere core competencies required to be considered a player.

Similar ≠ Same

CHAPTER 10

Discovering the
Consequences

"Let's move on to the second column: 'What are the consequences to the prospect in absence of each strength you identified in the column to the left?' List every consequence the prospect experiences in the absence of the strengths you identified in the left hand column."

Silence filled the room as Avery and Maria got to work on the middle column. I refilled our coffee mugs and thought about when I'd been starting out as a sales person. I remembered the time I was pursing a wonderful piece of new business and had superior technology and real DV in the way we serviced our accounts. Back then, I didn't have this process, so I just talked about how great our technology and service were. I was stuck in that first column and I wasn't differentiating very well at all.

In addition, my firm was a very new entrant into the IT sector. We were chasing a big sale and our main competition was fifty times my company's size. They were also touting their customer support advantage and they had many more experts potentially available to this customer. This competitor conveniently ignored the fact that their installed base was so full of creaking legacy systems that the experts were spending all their time keeping antiques running.

As we were in the final hours, I heard that the support issue was about to be fatal to my case. I knew the truth—the consequence of choosing my

What are the top five strengths or unique characteristics you offer to your ideal prospects?	What are all the consequences to the prospect in absence of each strength you identified in the column to the left?	Of all the consequences, which is most desirable? How do the consequences show up? Whose operating statement reflects them? Who gets the financial bill? (Emotional Customer)
1. _____ _____ _____ _____ _____	1. _____ _____ _____ _____ _____	1. _____ _____ _____ _____ _____
2. _____ _____ _____ _____ _____	2. _____ _____ _____ _____ _____	2. _____ _____ _____ _____ _____
3. _____ _____ _____ _____ _____	3. _____ _____ _____ _____ _____	3. _____ _____ _____ _____ _____
4. _____ _____ _____ _____ _____	4. _____ _____ _____ _____ _____	4. _____ _____ _____ _____ _____
5. _____ _____ _____ _____ _____	5. _____ _____ _____ _____ _____	5. _____ _____ _____ _____ _____

competitor—was that there would be poor to no support. I got a meeting with the decision maker and, sitting in his office, asked him to call the competition and ask a simple technical question, as a prospect. Then, call my company and compare the experience. I hadn't told anyone at my company that I'd be doing this, and he knew that.

When he called my competitor, he was put through an interrogation process, then handed off, given excuses and never given an answer. After 45 minutes on the phone, he was told they needed a purchase order for consulting as this would be billable time.

Then he called my company. He got his answer within five minutes.

Later that day, he made his decision public. When he called the sales person at my competitor, the sales person was already at his company's victory party, thinking they had this sale in the bag. That party turned into a wake.

That's when I learned the value of not talking about my DV as a list of qualities, but rather showing the consequences to the prospect of not having it. Now I had to bring Avery and Maria through the process of finding the consequences to their prospects.

When they stopped writing, I asked "What've we got?"

Avery spoke first. "Every day their new generic cereal isn't on store shelves, this company is losing millions of dollars. That's a huge consequence. Also, if they rush to market but the taste isn't right so consumers aren't buying, they're going to have to reformulate. That's after they realize sales are down, so that costs them in lost sales and again when they've got to pull food scientists off other projects to figure out why this new cereal isn't appealing to consumers."

"Great," I said. "Can you see how you can use this DV to alter the prospect or customer's decision-making process so that more value is placed on your competitive strengths than on things like price or fees?"

"Absolutely. Comparing 3 cents a pound for cinnamon to all that money they're going to lose if the new vendor can't get them to market as fast and with as good a product, well, they'd be losing a lot of money to save a little."

"Maria, what consequences did you find?"

"I talked about tracking lost leads before. Now I'm seeing that we could create our own measures to talk about what they could reasonably expect in terms of online leads. That way they'd feel the pain when they're not getting those new people. I realized that they really don't have benchmarks. They don't know what's possible. We work with a lot of firms like theirs, so we can show in hard numbers what they're missing by not moving forward with our solution."

Maria saw me nod and went on explaining, "Also there's something about reputation here. We really do have great people, but what that means for our clients is that they're spared embarrassment in the marketplace. We never let them go out there with outdated technology, for example. So when I say 'great people,' I'm really talking about how we protect our clients' reputations and brand."

"You're both getting ahead of me!" I said, grinning. "As you can see on the worksheet, we need to identify the most unprofitable or undesirable consequences that show up in the absence of your strengths. If your strengths have value for your prospects and customers, they are definitely going to experience an undesirable consequence. And you can see how the questions follow from that."

I'd written the questions from the DV sheet on the whiteboard, and now I pointed to it:

2: How do the consequences show up or manifest themselves?
3: Whose operating statement reflects that consequence?
4: Ultimately, who gets the total financial bill for it?

2: How do the consequences show up or manifest themselves?

3: Whose operating statement reflects that consequence?

4: Ultimately, who gets the total financial bill for it?

"On number four, that will be the Emotional Customer for sure. This would be the time to add the Emotional Customer to your contact or account management plan if they are not already in there. Or you might discover other Emotional Customers you hadn't seen when we first talked about this," I said.

I paused, making sure I had their attention, before adding, "You must know who feels the consequences the most, whether it's operationally, financially, market share, time to market, inability to attract key employees, or whatever unit of measure you want to use. You are identifying additional Emotional Customers, so you have a complete cast of characters and will win the 'economic democracy' election. The economic democracy is how I want you to think about the fact that the Emotional Customer gets many more votes than the logical. If the Logical Customer is saving their company $5,000, that's 5,000 votes, but if choosing the low-cost vendor ultimately costs their company $9 million, then the Emotional Customer has nine million votes. If you've communicated your consequences well, the decision makers will know who gets the lion's share of the votes."

"Wait a minute," Avery said. "Wouldn't I eventually just include everyone in that company as an Emotional Customer? If I keep going, I get to a point where the most undesirable consequence of not having us is that they go out of business. So then everyone takes the hit."

I nodded because a lot of people in my seminars came to that point and I was used to sending them in a more productive direction. "That might be true," I said. "But it is very hard to get the prospect to make the connection that far into the future and that far along the chain of consequence. That's more likely to end up with you in an argument with the prospect. A much easier path is to think about the short to medium-term stressful events, phone calls, work-arounds, angry conversations, lost revenue and opportunity that are created in the absence of your DV."

I added, "It's the description of those events and the open-ended questions that are attached that cause the Emotional and Logical Customers to be more open to a discussion about your DV. What you mentioned about lost time to market and product failure—that's a lot more important to your customer."

"This is a lot to think about," Maria said.

"I know. I've been thinking about it for decades," I told her. "And I've given you a lot today. You can go through this DV worksheet more than once. You'll learn more every time you run through this simple process of listing the strengths you think are unique or worth talking about, then working through in the middle column to identify every consequence you can come up with."

"Remember, in the far right-hand column, you get into your prospect's world, and you establish how those consequences show up and who feels them the most. You will have gone through the process of translating your Differentiating Value from an intellectual concept into emotional consequences that have far greater impact for those most concerned: the Emotional Customers in your prospect's organization."

CHAPTER 11

The Meeting After
the Meeting

"What if we have our consequences, but we're only talking to the Logical Customer? Are they going to care?" Avery asked.

"Fantastic question. Let me tell you where your consequences really come into play: at the meeting and after the meeting. In complex sales, which always involve multiple decision makers and multiple meetings, there are many meetings that happen after you meet with a prospect."

I went to the whiteboard and drew a rectangle for the conference table

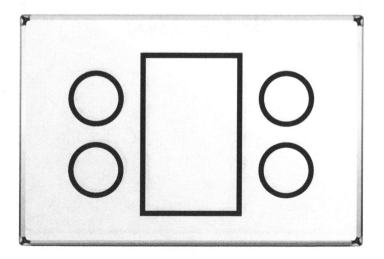

and circles on both sides of it. "I want you to envision a conference room with a table. On one side are your Emotional Customers and on the other side are the Logical Customers. What's important to the Logical Customers?"

"Price," Maria said. "They're getting rewarded for all the concessions they can get from us and the other vendors."

I nodded to her. "Exactly. Their bonuses may even be based on those discounts and concessions. Now on the other side of the table, the Emotional Customers want the best possible solutions and the lowest Total Cost of Ownership Over the Life™ of the solution—which we call the TCOOL.™ The Emotional Customers have to live with this thing once the deal is done, and it affects them for years."

I tapped the circles on one side of the table I'd drawn and then on the other. "You've got a long timeframe on one side and a shorter timeframe on the other. What everyone needs to understand is there are no free moves. All decisions involve tradeoffs, tradeoffs have consequences."

I wrote: *No free moves.*

"To determine the total cost of ownership over the life, the TCOOL,™ you have to add two sets of numbers: what you pay up front and what you'll pay over time. What you pay over time includes lost revenue from delayed time to market and missed sales. It's your job as the sales person to make sure that you understand the TCOOL™ and its impact on the Emotional Customer. You need to make sure the Emotional Customer can articulate the consequences of not

making TCOOL™ more important in their decision process."

"What if we have our consequences, but we're only talking to the Logical Customer?" Avery asked again.

"Your job is to pull the Emotional Customer's agenda into the conversation with the Logical Customer and make it very clear that they're talking about sacrificing TCOOL™ in order to get price concessions."

Maria was shaking her head. "But what if they think we're a commodity? For example, they think that any marketing firm can create a pretty good website. What if they don't see a difference in the TCOOL.™"

I said, "Then you have work to do. You have to walk them through it. Pretend you're one of your prospects and you've just told me that you think a new website is a commodity. I'd say, 'If it weren't a commodity, when would you want to know?'"

"Well now," she said, laughing a little and getting into the spirit of this impromptu role-playing. "But we're pretty sure it is a commodity. You'll have to prove it isn't."

I went on, "I wouldn't have brought it up if I couldn't prove it. Let's assume we prove it, then what?" I paused, breaking from my role as sales person to add, "See, I don't want to be doing that proof unless I know you're going to change your criteria so that you're not conflating price and cost. So I have to jump ahead and find out if that proof is going to make a difference to you. If it's not, then you're not a good prospect for me and I can stop wasting my time. Now, let's assume you tell me this proof will change your process, then I do the proof. How would you prove consequences to a prospect?"

Maria thought for a minute, rubbing her chin, and then said, "I'd say that in working with firms like theirs, we've seen a great website deliver twice as many leads as a mediocre site. And then I'd ask how many leads they get online now. They'll either give me a small number or zero. If they say it's zero I can say, 'Well, a firm your size should be expecting at least eight good online leads a month. What's your close rate?' And then I can calculate from their close rate how many clients that means, and they know the dollar value to them of a new client."

I told Maria and Avery, "A big component of cost is lost opportunities. And that will dwarf any concessions the Logical Customer can squeeze out of you. They're trying to get a six percent price concession while every day they're waiting for access to your DV they're losing thousands or millions of dollars.

Once you get all those hard numbers out on the table here's what I'd ask …

"How comfortable are you taking the revenue hit for the team?"

They both laughed appreciatively. "Great question," Avery said.

"You have to blow this up as the biggest scam that the Logical Customer runs," I said. "It's the ultimate cost shift—from the Logical Customer to the Emotional Customer—because the Logical Customer never pays for it. Maria, this is also how you can solve that problem about prospects going dark and never making a decision. Ask yourself: 'what's happening to whom because they're waiting?' They're sending you a message about their perceptions of the cost and consequences of waiting. What's that message?"

"That there aren't significant costs or consequences," she said.

"I've got news for you, if there are no costs or consequences, how long should they wait?"

Avery laughed and said, "Forever."

"Right. If that's true, they're not a good prospect for you. And if it's not true, and there are real consequences, you've got to get that cost of delay out on the table."

On the whiteboard, in the middle of the rectangular conference table, I put a dollar sign.

"Why don't you two go think about this more. Let's see how many of your problems are solved by what we've talked about today. Come back tomorrow afternoon and we'll do the last steps in messaging your DV to your customers and prospects."

CHAPTER 12

· ◀▬ ▶

Messaging Your Differentiating Value

"I found more consequences," Avery said brightly when we met the following afternoon. "But I can't imagine it's going to be very useful to just call up my former client and tell them—even if I do get the Emotional Customer on the phone."

Maria settled into her seat from the day before and said, "I remember in the bootcamp you said a lot about asking questions, but there was a process to that."

"Yes, let's look at the pieces of that process and then we'll put them together," I told them. "One of the benefits of focusing on consequences is that you can quickly craft components of your message and use the components to construct a phrase that will be useful in live conversation and electronic approach messages. Let me tell you a story:

> *One of our clients offers HVAC systems and services to commercial building owners. In conjunction with their maintenance service contracts, for several years they've invested in software to monitor points of failure in their customers' system components. As a result, our client has an increasingly accurate ability to predict when a critical piece of equipment will fail. When we were crafting the DV-based messaging, we identified clear consequences of not having evolving expertise and analytics.*

This had to do with Murphy's Law: that whatever can go wrong will do so at the worst possible time. Most breakdowns happen during peak demand and could have been accurately predicted and planned for.

The consequences were centered on being forced to deal with the outage reactively rather than proactively. Over time, we could decrease the frequency and duration of outages, impacting tenant satisfaction, resulting in fewer overtime charges for technicians and crisis avoidance.

Now we didn't want to just sell our client's cinnamon. So instead of talking about the consequences of not having their system, our client used approach messages like: "I may be contacting you a little too early. We help property owners who are open to reducing some of the drama, expense and negative tenant experience associated with system failures that could have been more accurately predicted and handled proactively. How open are you to a brief conversation to see if there is value for you in what we have learned?

I'd erased parts of the whiteboard from yesterday and added some new sections. I pointed to one section now and said, "Here are some of the DV components we've deployed to help many clients have the right conversations."

What the client gets with our DV	Consequences of going without our DV
Superior user experience	Takes longer to acquire fewer customers
Consistently achieve aggressive time to market goals	Launch date insecurity, revenue slips. unnecessary recovery expense
Decrease time to diagnose or resolve problems	Lower level of opportunities to sell
Integrated solution	Unnecessarily high TCOOL™

"Notice that the *consequences* point to the Emotional Customers, who have receptors for the pains of those consequences. When you create messages they connect with, it provides you an opportunity to *have* or *extend* sales conversations."

Maria had been nodding as she read down the list. She said, "It's great for marketing too. These are the kind of messages, both the DV and what happens when you don't have it, that we use in all kinds of marketing materials. Having them expressed well in our marketing makes it easier for sales because the prospects are already beginning to think about what makes us different and what can happen to them if they don't work with us."

Pointing to the bottom right section, I said, "Before we talk more about finding consequences, you can see that TCOOL™ is listed here. It could also be repeated in a number of these areas. And TCOOL™ is almost always the thing that Logical Customers want to keep out of the decision process, because if they get away with it, it's the ultimate cost shift to the Emotional Customer. The consequences are massive in terms of future pain to the organization. It shows up in an inability to renew major contracts, longer time to market—as we've already mentioned. Plus, it causes sales people trouble when trying to win new business because those short-term price concessions were great for the Logical Customer, but total costs were a disaster for the organization.

CHAPTER 13

· ━━ ▪

Finding Consequences

One of the biggest problems I see with the sales people I train is that they're not looking hard enough and uncovering all the consequences. I wanted to make sure that Maria and Avery really got this point. So I told them this story:

A few years ago, I had a client who made capital production equipment for very specialized, high tech assembly lines. My client shows up to a tradeshow one day and their most feared competitor is demonstrating a new piece of equipment that on the tradeshow floor is doing twice what my client's machine can do. My client had a 3,000 piece/hour run rate and this competitor is demonstrating, live, a 6,000 piece/hour rate.

The sales team wanted to go home and cry. But they came to me and I reminded them: there are no free moves. Nobody's changed the laws of physics. If that competitor is faster, they had to take that speed from somewhere else. All business decisions involve tradeoffs and they have consequences.

While the new machine looked invincible, we started to look at the tradeoffs the engineers made to demonstrate such amazing throughput. It turns out that they were achieving the blazing speed by running the same assembly over and over again. They could be incredibly fast only for huge lot sizes.

In the real world, only a fraction of the tech assembly work was like that. Most companies needed a machine like this for much smaller lot sizes; it took a lot of time to change over this new machine to handle each different assembly.

When we talked to actual users outside of the tradeshow, running in small lot sizes, they were only getting between 1,200 to 2,000 parts per hour on this competitor's machine.

It only took two questions for prospects to see what this would mean to them:

1. *"I'm sure that throughput is impressive. When you looked at the difference between your work and the demo, what did you learn?*
2. *"What would it mean to your business if your actual throughput was less than a third of the demonstration?"*

If my clients had stopped at the tradeshow demo and hadn't looked deeper, they wouldn't have found the real consequences of their customers investing in this flashy piece of equipment.

All business decisions involve tradeoffs and they have consequences.

CHAPTER 14

Using
Consequences
in Questions

Stepping back to the whiteboard, I told Avery and Maria, "Once you have clarity about the consequences of not having your DV, you can use a simple three-question sequence."

Knowing that we would talk about these today, I'd written them on the whiteboard and I pointed to the first one:

Question #1: "It varies from one customer to another as to what factors will be most important when picking a solution provider. What do you see being most important to your selection?"

I told them, "Almost always the answer will be core competencies such as service, support and price. Maria, your DV includes integrated delivery. What are the consequences of not having that?"

"Longer time to make changes to their website and online presence, which means missed leads and opportunities," she said. "It can also mean outdated marketing information going out from their firm and damaging their reputation."

"Avery, we talked about how the freshness of your cinnamon isn't the real DV. Your company provides expertise with the cinnamon that makes it much faster for their generics to reach supermarket shelves and sell well. What this customer is really missing is faster time to shelves and sales, right? In that case, you get to ask…" I pointed to:

Question #2: I notice you didn't mention speed of time to market with new generic cereal offerings. What should we assume about time to market in your selection of a supplier?

"Or, in your case, Maria, you might ask: 'I notice you didn't mention further reduction in leads and prospects due to outdated marketing efforts. What should we assume about those factors?'"

I let those questions sink in and then gave them the last question:

Question #3: "What if the solution that speeds time to market comes at a higher price than those who don't offer those capabilities?

Or: "What if the solution that brings you more leads, faster, and helps you close those sales has a higher price than those who don't offer those capabilities?"

"I like that," Maria said.

"It really does change how you think about it," Avery added.

"Right," I said, "The consequences were an unrecognized cost shift to the Emotional Customer. Often, the Emotional Customer has never been contacted by the sales person, and may be totally unaware that their interests are not being served by their own organization's buying process."

I explained, "This is the case in about 90% of the autopsies we do across all industries, where a high DV player should have won but did not win: they were not covering all the players in their cast of characters and as a result they did not understand how the decision would be made."

#1: "It varies from one customer to another as to what factors will be most important when picking a solution provider. What do you see being most important to your selection?"

#2: I notice you didn't mention speed of time to market with new generic cereal offerings. What should we assume about time to market in your selection of a supplier?

#3: "What if the solution that speeds time to market comes at a higher price than those who don't offer those capabilities?

SUMMARY

1. When you have clarity about your DV, you can leverage it effectively with the right people.

2. If you don't include both the Logical and Emotional Customers in your strategy, you will weaken your case and the yield from your business development process. It's difficult to win if you are working with an incomplete cast of characters.

3. As a high DV player, you cannot allow their buying process to equate price and the true total cost of not having your DV. You must master the conversation around price as a component of cost, and cost over time.

CHAPTER 15

Don't Talk About
Your DV,
Ask About It

It was time to wrap this up. "We're ready to finish this last step," I said. "You know your differentiating value and you know how to discover and communicate your DV to the Emotional Customer. I've seen over three decades of sales conversations—what do you think is the least effective way to communicate your DV to customers?"

"Hit them over the head with it?" Avery suggested.

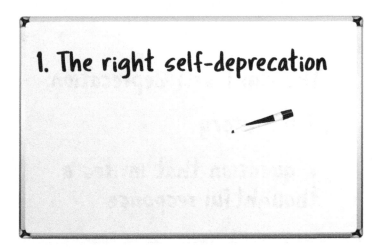

1. The right self-deprecation

"Essentially, yes. *Telling* customers about your company and your DV often looks like commercials produced and delivered by amateurs. Do not confuse telling them with selling! You're essentially joining the chorus of the thousands of messages they get every day about what they should be doing with their attention, their time and their money. You become clutter."

"But there's more to it than just asking questions, isn't there?" Maria asked. "I remember from your bootcamp, you want them to feel okay about the process and then there's a build up to the question."

"Open with the right blend of self-deprecation," I said. "For example, 'I may be bringing this up at the wrong time.'" I wrote on the whiteboard: *the right self-deprecation.*

"Then tell a relevant third-party *consequences* story. Every client I work with can come up with some events that happened to their customers or prospects that are true and show the consequences of not having their DV. Everyone loves stories. We spend billions a year to have people tell us stories!" I wrote this under the first line: Tell a story.

"Lastly, end with a question that invites a thoughtful response," I said and added that to the whiteboard.

The whiteboard looked like:

1. *The right self-deprecation*
2. *Tell a story*
3. *A question that invites a thoughtful response*

1. The right self-deprecation
2. Tell a story
3. A question that invites a thoughtful response

"Let me give you an example from my business. I will often say something like, 'I'm not sure I'm bringing this up at the right time. I'm fortunate to have hundreds of conversations a year with CEOs and business owners. One of the things they are very vocal about is how hard it is to find and keep stronger sales people. How open are you to a brief conversation to see if what we've learned helping hundreds of companies with that problem might have value for you?'"

I sensed that Maria and Avery needed to better understand the gap, so I told them, "When I talk about how hard it is to find and keep stronger sales people –that evokes the gap between where they are versus where they could be if they had access to what we know. Our knowledge and experience are components of our DV, and without them it's harder to solve a universal problem. Aren't consequences fun? A 'brief conversation' indicates I'm not about to educate or solve the prospect's problem for free."

"The phrase, 'might have value for you' indicates that we may not be a fit, and it's ok if this conversation does not go anywhere. My marketing mentors have taught me that people tend to be more interested in that which they may not be able to have."

SUMMARY

1. **Telling** prospects about your DV makes you part of the clutter.

2. Tell stories and ask questions that uncover the consequences of not having your DV.

CHAPTER 16

How Did
It End?

A lthough Avery and Maria's names are fictional, this book is inspired by true stories from my clients. In the real cinnamon story, $1,200 of annual savings on ingredient price paled compared to the exposure to a $10 million revenue hit that came with the $1,200 savings.

Avery and I rehearsed a voicemail he would leave. He'd identified his Emotional Customer: the product line manager. We refined his message to include his DV. It had to be a voicemail, not email, because we needed the tonality and cadence of a voice message.

The message was: "Hi, this is Avery Davis. We may not need to talk in person. I understand your company has decided to add three weeks' time to market to the rollout of new products.

That seems to be a change in strategy with some consequences. If you'd like the three weeks back, I can be reached at 952-123-1234"

Notice that he wasn't talking about cinnamon. He talked about the consequences of not buying his cinnamon, that is the consequence of not having his DV: longer time to market.

That voicemail triggered internal meetings about how to minimize the damage to top-line revenue and market share, until the contract with the new supplier ran out.

In addition, they agreed to pay Avery a consulting fee until they could redirect the business back to him.

Like most salespeople, Avery has a very strong need to be liked (50% of sales people do) and the buyer was very unhappy with him. I explained the buyer was just doing his job and that if Avery was looking for a friend, he should get a dog.

To my knowledge, Avery didn't get a dog. But he did get that client back when their contract with the new supplier ran out.

Maria had tools she could use with many stalled prospect conversations, but let's look at one in particular. A mid-sized firm needed a new website but felt the old one was working well enough that they didn't have to pull the trigger any time soon.

In order to prove consequences, Maria and her team persuaded this firm to show them their website analytics. They dug into the data and pointed to places where visitors were dropping off this firm's website. Using their benchmarking data, they had a pretty good idea of the potential leads and new clients who weren't coming in the door because the old site was hard to navigate and didn't lead these prospects to take action.

Putting the cost of a new site next to the question, "How much is a new client worth to you?"—and the realization that they were losing more in lost clients than they saved by waiting to start the new site design—got Maria's prospect eager to get to work with her firm. They not only signed the contract within a week, but they were fast about getting Maria's company the materials they needed to go to work on the new site.

If you are the high DV player, there is always a difference between price and true total cost. Your life improves dramatically when you use that difference to alter your prospect's decision process.

If you lead your company's sales team, it's your job to make sure they position themselves correctly, that they call on the **Emotional Customer**, and that they talk about the right things to the **Emotional Customer**. If you're the sales person, you will usually talk to both the **Emotional** and **Logical** Customer. It will always help, especially if you're a high Differentiating Value player, to focus on the **Emotional Customer**.

My challenge to you is this: When you understand the concept of your Differentiating Value and how it shows up in the life of your prospect when they don't have it, you gain more efficient use of your resources, reduce the length of your sales cycle and improve your margins. How long can you afford to wait for that change?

SUMMARY

You do not have to match the price of a competitor who does not have your DV if you can articulate your DV so the prospect understands your value.

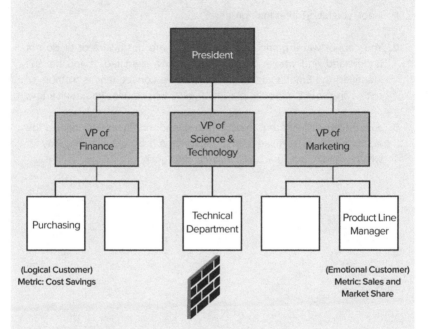

Isolation is the distance between a bad decision by the Logical Customer and the painful consequences to the Emotional Customer.

SUMMARY

1. If their processes for evaluating your offer do not include appropriate weight on your differentiators, you will need low price to win. Will that work for you?

   If not, you MUST alter their process.

2. You cannot win a game whose rules you are not aware of or do not understand and whose players you haven't identified. If you haven't identified the Emotional Customers and the consequences to them of not having your DV, you're playing a game whose rules you don't know.

3. Just because they are threatening to spend money in your part of the economy does not make them a prospect. A prospect is a company for which your DV would actually make a difference.

BONUS CHAPTER

Keeping Access To the Executive Decision Maker

A very and Maria, and many other clients like them, come to my office repeatedly over the years to fine tune their sales process and find more consequences that they're missing. Over time, most clients also want to find better ways to show their prospects the consequences of not having their DV. Communicating about DV is an ongoing process and often when you're inside your company, you're too close to what you do to see all the ways you can leverage your DV in sales conversations.

Just one of the many follow-up meetings I have is about keeping communication channels open with the Emotional Customer so you can prevent the DV erosion that happens naturally with time. I'm including that lesson below. If you have questions or are struggling to use your DV effectively in sales, please check online at www.slatterysales.com or www.whatwouldterrydo.com for more information learned from my decades of working with sales people like you.

Here's one of the next steps to practice after you get good at asking questions that prove your DV to the right prospect:

One of the most effective ways to maintain access to the decision maker (the Emotional Customer who awarded you the business) is to set an alarm in your calendar to go back to the decision-maker 30-60 days after your implementation team has verified that you have exceeded the client's original expectations.

———————

(There is nothing memorable for your client and you won't get a good reference if you merely meet expectations or fulfill a contract.)

When you know you've outperformed the spec, you get back in front of the executive and you have a conversation that sounds like this:

"When we were selected to help you solve the problem, we understood that your highest priorities were A, B, and C.

Our implementation team has confirmed with your people that we've met A and exceeded B and C.

Of course, that means nothing if that's not how you see it. What's your view of how many of your priorities have been addressed?"

I've had hundreds of reports from clients who have done this, and the reports say:

1. The executive is often surprised that the supplier brought closure with the original decision maker. Many times we've heard "nobody's ever done that with me."
2. They often bring up a related opportunity in the early stages, and we get a preview of how to position any applicable DV, before requirements are set in stone.
3. They also sometimes refer us to a colleague at another firm or business unit in their firm.

All of this from simply confirming that we did what they wanted and a little more.

I want to tell you one more story about a lesson that I learned, because I'm constantly learning too.

In my sales trainings over the years and the hundreds of companies we've worked with, we've seen that DV will illuminate your target in a competitive battle. It will light up that target and provide language for you to use to position yourself very effectively against your competitors' deficiencies.

I was working with a client who is a global manufacturer of industrial and medical products. I'd worked with the sales team for this product line about two years earlier, and during that time, they'd learned the basics of DV. We'd created the language on how to deploy their DV effectively in their marketplace and they were getting better results in profit margins and in their hit rate on proposals.

My client knew the basics of DV, but in the time that had elapsed since our initial work, a much larger competitor with a much bigger market share was deeply discounting some products as a defensive measure. This competitor was working hard to make their products financially attractive—and their products were more mature.

We knew that we had *Total Cost of Ownership Over The Life*™ of the system *(T.C.O.O.L.*™*)* as our most positive factor against the larger competitor's more attractive price and very appealing terms. But my client was having a challenge getting the prospect to recognize their real lower TCOOL™ advantage and to drive it into the evaluation and decision criteria as a "must-have."

When I got the phone call, the question from the sales leader with whom I had worked previously was, "How long would it take you to paint a bull's eye on my competitor, Brand X?" As he described the problem, my response was, "It'll take about four hours and…" I quoted my standard fee.

He came back to me shortly and said, "We're going to do it in Minneapolis and we're bringing in the president of our business to the meeting. He lives in Europe, but he is coming to Minneapolis for this meeting."

When I backgrounded the president, it turned out he has a PhD in physics, which is very appropriate for the kind of products we were working with. He has an elite MBA. He's multilingual, he's very smart, and he's very successful.

The meeting was in the hotel near the Minneapolis Airport. It opened with them describing the situation in more specific detail than they had on the initial phone call.

I responded with four questions whose answers would provide us with direction to leverage their DV. Because they already knew the principles of DV, I did not have to teach them DV. I just needed to update them for this specific competitive situation.

As you read this book, you saw these four questions woven into the text. I asked them:

1. "What's going to happen to whom if they don't have access to your DV?"
2. "How will it show up?"
3. "When will it show up?"
4. "Who gets the bill if it turns out that you were the better buy and yet they bought from the competition?"

In essence, what we were working through was the simple (but not easy) principle that if your differentiators have value, then not having them must have consequences. The four questions were meant to highlight the consequences.

It only took about four hours to strike gold. We came up with the essential questions that they needed to ask in their sales cycle to begin to drive their DV into the customer's decision process, tilting the competitive playing field toward my client.

When the meeting concluded, I was giving the president a 10-minute ride back to the Minneapolis Airport so he could catch the next flight home. He asked, "How much did you charge us for this meeting?"

I told him the price, which he would soon know because he was going to see the authorization for payment coming through shortly. He slapped his hand on the dash of my vehicle and said, "That's the problem!"

I asked, "What do you mean?"

He replied, "I have been talking with my North American sales team about this problem for the past several months, and they told me there was a person in Minneapolis who could help us solve this problem. But when I asked them, 'What does he charge?' they came back to me and told me the number, and I said, 'He can't know what he's doing. For a problem this big, you charge a lot more money.'"

Despite my low price, they came for the meeting.

My vehicle approached the terminal building. By now we had a good enough relationship that I could do this in good humor: as the vehicle stopped, I locked the door.

I said, "I'll unlock this door as soon as you tell me what the price is that would have told you instantly that I really had a solution and I knew what I was doing, since my price was too low and delayed this meeting?"

"I'm not going to tell you your price, but I am going to tell you that I routinely pay big-name consulting firms for help solving problems like this between eight and ten times what you just charged me.

"What you need to understand is that we'll make hundreds of millions with this information and tactics. You need to raise your prices because we may have this problem again, and I need to make sure you're still in business."

There's more to the story. A few months later, I was sharing a anonymized version of this story in a presentation to a CEO peer group in another state. One of the CEOs in the peer group came up to me after my presentation.

He said, "I think your client in the story you just told was ..." and he named the company. Then he said, "and I think the competitor that you targeted was..." and he named the target.

In competitive strategy DV work, I operate under strict nondisclosure agreements. I was surprised at his very accurate "guesses." Not only hadn't I named the companies, but I'd left out any possible identifying information.

I said: "That's a very interesting pair of guesses. Tell me more."

"My son is the product line manager for the competitor your client targeted. Your client took so many sales away from them and hit them so hard in that segment of their business that to stop the bleeding they had to announce a product that was not ready for delivery. They spent a fortune to keep the new product on the order books for many months until it could perform as planned."

He grinned when I asked: "Isn't it a small world?"

Shortly after that presentation, I raised my prices. I must not have raised them high enough because nobody yelled. What's interesting is that it now takes less time for the customer to make a decision to engage us, so apparently we're in the price ballpark we're supposed to play in. But price is hardly the whole story. I use the principles and practices around DV and consequences all the time in my own sales process.

My hope is you have enjoyed The Cinnamon Story and that you will find ways to apply the concepts in this book to your business to great success.

Thank you.

— Terry Slattery

Now what?

The concepts explained in this simple business fable are real. They are the result of years of work with more than 2,000 clients — professionals to Fortune-ranked international corporations — since 1985. The vision of Slattery Sales Group is to fully empower sales people to win at complex sales…and we do. Learn the secrets of winning at complex sales at www.whatwouldterrydo.com

If your corporate sales force is ready to increase margins, help your top line, shorten your sales cycle and respond quickly to competitive threats, contact us at:

Slattery Sales Group
952.832.5436
info@slatterysales.com
www.slatterysales.com

Made in the USA
Monee, IL
25 March 2024

55763027R00039